REDACTED ~~BLACKOUT~~

POETRY JOURNAL

Create Blackout Poetry by

Destroying the Classics

Offbeat Poet

Redacted Poetry Journal: *Create Blackout Poetry by Destroying the Classics*

Copyright © 2019 by Sherry Hale (Offbeat Poet)

All rights reserved. This book or any portion thereof may not be reproduced or used in any manner whatsoever without the express written permission of the publisher except for the use of brief quotations in a book review or scholarly journal. The excerpts of public domain works included in this journal were deemed free of copyright when accessed from the U.S.A. on May 1st 2019.

ISBN-13: 978-1725965553

ISBN-10: 1725965550

Written & Created by: Sherry Hale, Offbeat Poet

Published by: Melographics

RedactedPoetry.com // offbeatpoet.com

Table of Contents

THE POETIC ART OF REDACTION
- Getting Started
- Make it R.A.I.N. Redacted Poetry

READY FOR REDACTION (LITERATURE EXCERPTS)
- The Time Machine by H.G. Wells
- Peter Pan by James M. Barrie
- The Republic by Plato
- The Hound of the Baskervilles by Arthur Conan Doyle
- As You Like It by William Shakespeare
- The Wonderful Wizard of Oz by L. Frank Baum
- Candide by Voltaire
- David Copperfield by Charles Dickens
- Little Women by Louisa May Alcott
- The Strange Case of Dr. Jekyll & Mr. Hyde by Robert Louis Stevenson
- The Kama Sutra of Vatsyayana by Vatsyayana
- The Divine Comedy by Dante Alighieri
- Prudence, Essays by Ralph Waldo Emerson
- The War of the Worlds by H. G. Wells
- Treasure Island by Robert Louis Stevenson
- Ulysses by James Joyce

Redacted Poetry Journal

- Anne of Green Gables by Lucy Maud Montgomery
- Song of Myself, Leaves of Grass by Walt Whitman
- The Federalist Papers by Alexander Hamilton, John Jay, & James Madison
- Wuthering Heights by Emily Bronte
- Pride and Prejudice by Jane Austen
- Alice's Adventures in Wonderland by Lewis Carroll
- Moby Dick By Herman Melville
- The Adventures of Sherlock Holmes by Arthur Conan Doyle
- The Adventures of Tom Sawyer by Mark Twain
- Dracula by Bram Stoker
- A Tale of Two Cities by Charles Dickens
- Heart of Darkness by Joseph Conrad
- The Golden Bird, Grimms' Fairy Tales by The Brothers Grimm
- The Iliad of Homer by Homer
- War and Peace by Leo Tolstoy
- Frankenstein by Mary Wollstonecraft Shelley
- The Count of Monte Cristo by Alexandre Dumas, père
- The Importance of Being Earnest: A Trivial Comedy for Serious People by Oscar Wilde

- The Fall of the House of Usher by Edgar Allan Poe
- This Side of Paradise by F. Scott Fitzgerald
- Les Misérables by Victor Hugo
- Paradise Lost by John Milton
- Gulliver's Travels by Jonathan Swift
- The Call of the Wild by Jack London
- Hamlet by William Shakespeare
- Anthem by Ayn Rand
- The Tale of Peter Rabbit by Beatrix Potter
- Around the World in 80 Days by Jules Verne
- Utopia by Thomas More
- Twelve Years a Slave by Solomon Northup
- A Little Princess by Frances Hodgson Burnett
- The Almost-Men by Irving E. Cox
- The Waste Land by T. S. Eliot
- The Secret Garden by Frances Hodgson Burnett

Resources & Info

The Poetic Art of Redaction

Creativity Meets

a small child,

with

inspiration

support

and
love

Creativity by Sherry Hale

Redacted Poetry Journal

Getting Started

If imitation is the sincerest form of flattery; what is destruction? POETRY! Redacted poetry, a.k.a. blackout poetry, is a form of found poetry created by *finding* words within existing text and *redacting*, or removing, the rest. Redacted poetry is a series of decisions, like choosing the players on your team who will come together and achieve something greater than themselves.

From newspapers and magazines to books and letters; anything with words can be redacted. While periodicals are easy to find and disposable; there's a deeper, almost nostalgic, force that flows through poetry that is redacted from literature, especially the classic literature. As a book lover myself, the very thought of destroying a

Redacted Poetry Journal

physical piece literature felt criminal, ergo this Redacted Poetry Journal.

With ready to redact text in hand, you must trust yourself. Know that the poetic lines are hidden amongst the cluttered text and pages; waiting for your extraction through surgical redaction. Sometimes you may look at the page and instantly see the captive words screaming out with piercing clarity. While other times, you may just see a bunch of words. Struggling to declutter the page *and your mind* feels like trying to fill a net with water. IT'S OKAY! Don't pressure yourself to create something perfect. Just let go.

Whether this is your first time learning of redacted poetry, or you've redacted thousands of page; this Redacted Poetry Journal is here to help you rework, reimage, and reconnect with literary arts in a new way. As you continue to practice the art, you find methods and your own approach that best suits your creative process. But, for now, you can try my R.A.I.N. method for unleashing your redacted poetry flow. The framework listed below is simply a list of the steps I take when creating redacted poetry. You may find it helpful, or just more clutter. Feel free to steal whichever parts work for you—and blackout the rest.

Make it R.A.I.N. Redacted Poetry

On your mark(er). Get set. Go! Here's what you'll need to get started… *whatever you want*. No, seriously. If you want to use pens, pencils, markers, paint, scissors, or tape; it's up to you. I tend to take the minimalist approach and use a pencil and a black art marker (that doesn't bleed). The good news is that there are no "rules" you have to follow. Try different materials and supplies to fine what works best for you. As for your medium, it's in your hands! The following 100 pages include excerpts of classic works from some of the greatest writers of all time. Each page is cleanly formatted with extra white space for thoughts, notes, or nothing at all. Here are some steps to get started on your first redacted work of art.

READ: Skim over the page before you begin meticulously reading it through word for word. Be on the lookout for any words that jump right off of the page, or really resonate with you. You're looking for an anchor which is a main idea or subject that you can hold on to and expand on for your redacted poem. Identifying your anchor word creates clarity and perspective for the poem's tone, and theme. Relating your poem to the message of the original text is not important, nor necessary.

ANCHOR: Now that you have your anchor word, read the entire page from top to bottom. Proceed to circle any word that connects to your anchor word with a pencil. Make sure the words you circle are words that strike a chord within you. Refrain from circling more than two consecutive words.

INVENTORY: For this step you can either work straight out of the circled text, or for clarity, take out a separate sheet of paper and list out all the words you've circled in the exact same order that they have occurred on the page. This is very important. The arrangement of the words in a redacted poem must not change. As you're reviewing your selected words.

NIX: From the list or circled text, piece the words together in order top to bottom. Since redacted poems use the existing text, you will not be able to easily link a work from the bottom of the page to the top. Creatively, you can always create arrows or other visual ways not following the traditional flow, however, this often leads to confusion by the reader and dilutes the message.

    As you're piecing together your poem, feel free to eliminate entire words or portions of words (e.g. -ed, re-, -ing, de-) if it better crafts your message. With your final words chosen, return to the original text and "nix" the rest to uncover your redacted poem. You can use a marker, pen or pencil, depending on the visual look you're after.

📎 **TIP:** You can always return to the original text page if you find yourself stuck at this step. You might just find the right word waiting for you.

For those wanting to amplify their redacted poem and connect visual with literal meaning. Elevate your R.A.I.N. poem to a stunning R.A.I.N.E.D. work of art by adding "-E.D." (emphasize, decorate).

EMPHASIZE: On the original text; circle, box, or highlight the words you've chosen to survive as your redacted poem. By visually emphasizing the words you feel are most significant to your poem, you enhance the emotional effect of your prose.

DECORATE: Redacted poems do not have to be redacted in with black. Use other materials and mediums like colored pencils, paint, and crayons. Add doodles, illustrations, or visual elements to create a true work of art.

EXPLORE: This is *your* Redacted Poetry Journal. Black it out. Tear it up. Color it in. Follow my R.A.I.N. framework or find your own approach. Your only objective is to be creative; whatever that means to you. If you're open to sharing your work, I'd love to "like" it on social (Offbeat Poet). Visit **www.offbeatpoet.com** for ideas, tools, and tips. I look forward to seeing your #redactedpoetry works. Thank you for purchasing this Redacted Poetry Journal.

Cheers to creativity!

Ready for Redaction

Redacted Poetry Journal

The Time Machine by H.G. Wells

The thing the Time Traveller held in his hand was a glittering metallic framework, scarcely larger than a small clock, and very delicately made. There was ivory in it, and some transparent crystalline substance. And now I must be explicit, for this that follows—unless his explanation is to be accepted—is an absolutely unaccountable thing. He took one of the small octagonal tables that were scattered about the room, and set it in front of the fire, with two legs on the hearthrug. On this table he placed the mechanism. Then he drew up a chair, and sat down. The only other object on the table was a small shaded lamp, the bright light of which fell upon the model. There were also perhaps a dozen candles about, two in brass candlesticks upon the mantel and several in sconces, so that the room was brilliantly illuminated. I sat in a low

---

Redacted Poetry Journal

Peter Pan by James M. Barrie

All children, except one, grow up. They soon know that they will grow up, and the way Wendy knew was this. One day when she was two years old she was playing in a garden, and she plucked another flower and ran with it to her mother. I suppose she must have looked rather delightful, for Mrs. Darling put her hand to her heart and cried, "Oh, why can't you remain like this for ever!" This was all that passed between them on the subject, but henceforth Wendy knew that she must grow up. You always know after you are two. Two is the beginning of the end. Of course they lived at 14 [their house number on their street], and until Wendy came her mother was the chief one. She was a lovely lady, with a romantic mind and such a sweet mocking mouth. Her romantic mind was like the tiny boxes, one within the other, that come from the puzzling East

---

Redacted Poetry Journal

The Republic by Plato

I replied: There is nothing which for my part I like better, Cephalus, than conversing with aged men; for I regard them as travellers who have gone a journey which I too may have to go, and of whom I ought to enquire, whether the way is smooth and easy, or rugged and difficult. And this is a question which I should like to ask of you who have arrived at that time which the poets call the 'threshold of old age'—Is life harder towards the end, or what report do you give of it? I will tell you, Socrates, he said, what my own feeling is. Men of my age flock together; we are birds of a feather, as the old proverb says; and at our meetings the tale of my acquaintance commonly is—I cannot eat, I cannot drink; the pleasures of youth and love are fled away: there was a good time once, but now that is gone, and life is no longer life. Some complain of

Redacted Poetry Journal

The Hound of the Baskervilles

by Arthur Conan Doyle

The train pulled up at a small wayside station and we all descended. Outside, beyond the low, white fence, a wagonette with a pair of cobs was waiting. Our coming was evidently a great event, for station-master and porters clustered round us to carry out our luggage. It was a sweet, simple country spot, but I was surprised to observe that by the gate there stood two soldierly men in dark uniforms who leaned upon their short rifles and glanced keenly at us as we passed. The coachman, a hard-faced, gnarled little fellow, saluted Sir Henry Baskerville, and in a few minutes we were flying swiftly down the broad, white road. Rolling pasture lands curved upward on either side of us, and old gabled houses peeped out from amid the thick green foliage, but behind the peaceful and sunlit countryside there rose ever, dark against the evening sky,

Redacted Poetry Journal

As You Like It by William Shakespeare

DUKE SENIOR. Now, my co-mates and brothers in exile, Hath not old custom made this life more sweet. Than that of painted pomp? Are not these woods. More free from peril than the envious court? Here feel we not the penalty of Adam, The seasons' difference; as the icy fang And churlish chiding of the winter's wind, Which when it bites and blows upon my body, Even till I shrink with cold, I smile and say This is no flattery; these are counsellors That feelingly persuade me what I am.' Sweet are the uses of adversity, Which, like the toad, ugly and venomous, Wears yet a precious jewel in his head; And this our life, exempt from public haunt, Finds tongues in trees, books in the running brooks, Sermons in stones, and good in everything I would not change it. AMIENS. Happy is your Grace, That can translate the stubbornness of fortune

Redacted Poetry Journal

The Wonderful Wizard of Oz by L. Frank Baum

Dorothy lived in the midst of the great Kansas prairies, with Uncle Henry, who was a farmer, and Aunt Em, who was the farmer's wife. Their house was small, for the lumber to build it had to be carried by wagon many miles. There were four walls, a floor and a roof, which made one room; and this room contained a rusty looking cookstove, a cupboard for the dishes, a table, three or four chairs, and the beds. Uncle Henry and Aunt Em had a big bed in one corner, and Dorothy a little bed in another corner. There was no garret at all, and no cellar--except a small hole dug in the ground, called a cyclone cellar, where the family could go in case one of those great whirlwinds arose, mighty enough to crush any building in its path. It was reached by a trap door in the middle of the floor, from which a ladder led down into the small, dark hole. When Dorothy

---

Redacted Poetry Journal

Candide by Voltaire

Half dead of that inconceivable anguish which the rolling of a ship produces, one-half of the passengers were not even sensible of the danger. The other half shrieked and prayed. The sheets were rent, the masts broken, the vessel gaped. Work who would, no one heard, no one commanded. The Anabaptist being upon deck bore a hand; when a brutish sailor struck him roughly and laid him sprawling; but with the violence of the blow he himself tumbled head foremost overboard, and stuck upon a piece of the broken mast. Honest James ran to his assistance, hauled him up, and from the effort he made was precipitated into the sea in sight of the sailor, who left him to perish, without deigning to look at him. Candide drew near and saw his benefactor, who rose above the water one moment and was then swallowed up for ever. He was just going to jump after

Redacted Poetry Journal

David Copperfield by Charles Dickens

The first objects that assume a distinct presence before me, as I look far back, into the blank of my infancy, are my mother with her pretty hair and youthful shape, and Peggotty with no shape at all, and eyes so dark that they seemed to darken their whole neighbourhood in her face, and cheeks and arms so hard and red that I wondered the birds didn't peck her in preference to apples. I believe I can remember these two at a little distance apart, dwarfed to my sight by stooping down or kneeling on the floor, and I going unsteadily from the one to the other. I have an impression on my mind which I cannot distinguish from actual remembrance, of the touch of Peggotty's forefinger as she used to hold it out to me, and of its being roughened by needlework, like a pocket nutmeg-grater. This may be fancy, though I think the memory of most

---

Redacted Poetry Journal

Little Women by Louisa May Alcott

As young readers like to know 'how people look', we will take this moment to give them a little sketch of the four sisters, who sat knitting away in the twilight, while the December snow fell quietly without, and the fire crackled cheerfully within. It was a comfortable room, though the carpet was faded and the furniture very plain, for a good picture or two hung on the walls, books filled the recesses, chrysanthemums and Christmas roses bloomed in the windows, and a pleasant atmosphere of home peace pervaded it. Margaret, the eldest of the four, was sixteen, and very pretty, being plump and fair, with large eyes, plenty of soft brown hair, a sweet mouth, and white hands, of which she was rather vain. Fifteen-year-old Jo was very tall, thin, and brown, and reminded one of a colt, for she never seemed to know what to do with her long limbs,

---

Redacted Poetry Journal

The Strange Case of Dr. Jekyll & Mr. Hyde

by Robert Louis Stevenson

Mr. Utterson the lawyer was a man of a rugged countenance that was never lighted by a smile; cold, scanty and embarrassed in discourse; backward in sentiment; lean, long, dusty, dreary and yet somehow lovable. At friendly meetings, and when the wine was to his taste, something eminently human beaconed from his eye; something indeed which never found its way into his talk, but which spoke not only in these silent symbols of the after-dinner face, but more often and loudly in the acts of his life. He was austere with himself; drank gin when he was alone, to mortify a taste for vintages; and though he enjoyed the theatre, had not crossed the doors of one for twenty years. But he had an approved tolerance for others; sometimes wondering, almost with envy, at the high pressure of spirits involved in their misdeeds; and in any extremity inclined

The Kama Sutra of Vatsyayana by Vatsyayana

But Vatsyayana is of opinion that this objection does not hold good, for women already know the practice of Kama Sutra, and that practice is derived from the Kama Shastra, or the science of Kama itself. Moreover, it is not only in this but in many other cases that though the practice of a science is known to all, only a few persons are acquainted with the rules and laws on which the science is based. Thus the Yadnikas or sacrificers, though ignorant of grammar, make use of appropriate words when addressing the different Deities, and do not know how these words are framed. Again, persons do the duties required of them on auspicious days, which are fixed by astrology, though they are not acquainted with the science of astrology. In a like manner riders of horses and elephants train these animals without knowing the science of training

The Divine Comedy by Dante Alighieri

His glory, by whose might all things are mov'd, Pierces the universe, and in one part Sheds more resplendence, elsewhere less. In heav'n, That largeliest of his light partakes, was I, Witness of things, which to relate again Surpasseth power of him who comes from thence; For that, so near approaching its desire Our intellect is to such depth absorb'd, That memory cannot follow. Nathless all, That in my thoughts I of that sacred realm Could store, shall now be matter of my song. Benign Apollo! this last labour aid, And make me such a vessel of thy worth, As thy own laurel claims of me belov'd. Thus far hath one of steep Parnassus' brows Suffic'd me; henceforth there is need of both For my remaining enterprise Do thou Enter into my bosom, and there breathe So, as when Marsyas by thy hand was dragg'd Forth from his limbs unsheath'd. O power divine! If

Prudence, Essays by Ralph Waldo Emerson

What right have I to write on Prudence, whereof I have little, and that of the negative sort? My prudence consists in avoiding and going without, not in the inventing of means and methods, not in adroit steering, not in gentle repairing. I have no skill to make money spend well, no genius in my economy, and whoever sees my garden discovers that I must have some other garden. Yet I love facts, and hate lubricity and people without perception. Then I have the same title to write on prudence that I have to write on poetry or holiness. We write from aspiration and antagonism, as well as from experience. We paint those qualities which we do not possess. The poet admires the man of energy and tactics; the merchant breeds his son for the church or the bar; and where a man is not vain and egotistic you shall find what he has not by his praise. Moreover

The War of the Worlds by H. G. Wells

No one would have believed in the last years of the nineteenth century that this world was being watched keenly and closely by intelligences greater than man's and yet as mortal as his own; that as men busied themselves about their various concerns they were scrutinised and studied, perhaps almost as narrowly as a man with a microscope might scrutinise the transient creatures that swarm and multiply in a drop of water. With infinite complacency men went to and fro over this globe about their little affairs, serene in their assurance of their empire over matter. It is possible that the infusoria under the microscope do the same. No one gave a thought to the older worlds of space as sources of human danger, or thought of them only to dismiss the idea of life upon them as impossible or improbable. It is curious to recall some of the

Treasure Island by Robert Louis Stevenson

He was a very silent man by custom. All day he hung round the cove or upon the cliffs with a brass telescope; all evening he sat in a corner of the parlour next the fire and drank rum and water very strong. Mostly he would not speak when spoken to, only look up sudden and fierce and blow through his nose like a fog-horn; and we and the people who came about our house soon learned to let him be. Every day when he came back from his stroll he would ask if any seafaring men had gone by along the road. At first we thought it was the want of company of his own kind that made him ask this question, but at last we began to see he was desirous to avoid them. When a seaman did put up at the Admiral Benbow (as now and then some did, making by the coast road for Bristol) he would look in at him through the curtained door before he entered the parlour; and he was

Ulysses by James Joyce

He watched her pour into the measure and thence into the jug rich white milk, not hers. Old shrunken paps. She poured again a measureful and a tilly. Old and secret she had entered from a morning world, maybe a messenger. She praised the goodness of the milk, pouring it out. Crouching by a patient cow at daybreak in the lush field, a witch on her toadstool, her wrinkled fingers quick at the squirting dugs. They lowed about her whom they knew, dewsilky cattle. Silk of the kine and poor old woman, names given her in old times. A wandering crone, lowly form of an immortal serving her conqueror and her gay betrayer, their common cuckquean, a messenger from the secret morning. To serve or to upbraid, whether he could not tell: but scorned to beg her favour.
—It is indeed, ma'am, Buck Mulligan said, pouring milk into their cups.

Anne of Green Gables by Lucy Maud Montgomery

Mrs. Rachel Lynde lived just where the Avonlea main road dipped down into a little hollow, fringed with alders and ladies' eardrops and traversed by a brook that had its source away back in the woods of the old Cuthbert place; it was reputed to be an intricate, headlong brook in its earlier course through those woods, with dark secrets of pool and cascade; but by the time it reached Lynde's Hollow it was a quiet, well-conducted little stream, for not even a brook could run past Mrs. Rachel Lynde's door without due regard for decency and decorum; it probably was conscious that Mrs. Rachel was sitting at her window, keeping a sharp eye on everything that passed, from brooks and children up, and that if she noticed anything odd or out of place she would never rest until she had ferreted out the whys and wherefores thereof. There are plenty of people in

Song of Myself, Leaves of Grass

by Walt Whitman

I celebrate myself, and sing myself, And what I assume you shall assume, For every atom belonging to me as good belongs to you. I loafe and invite my soul, I lean and loafe at my ease observing a spear of summer grass. My tongue, every atom of my blood, form'd from this soil, this air, Born here of parents born here from parents the same, and their parents the same,I, now thirty-seven years old in perfect health begin, Hoping to cease not till death. Creeds and schools in abeyance, Retiring back a while sufficed at what they are, but never forgotten, I harbor for good or bad, I permit to speak at every hazard, Nature without check with original energy. Houses and rooms are full of perfumes, the shelves are crowded with perfumes, I breathe the fragrance myself and know it and like it, The distillation would intoxicate me

Redacted Poetry Journal

The Federalist Papers by Alexander Hamilton, John Jay, & James Madison

After an unequivocal experience of the inefficacy of the subsisting federal government, you are called upon to deliberate on a new Constitution for the United States of America. The subject speaks its own importance; comprehending in its consequences nothing less than the existence of the UNION, the safety and welfare of the parts of which it is composed, the fate of an empire in many respects the most interesting in the world. It has been frequently remarked that it seems to have been reserved to the people of this country, by their conduct and example, to decide the important question, whether societies of men are really capable or not of establishing good government from reflection and choice, or whether they are forever destined to depend for their political constitutions on accident and force. If there be any truth in the re-

Wuthering Heights by Emily Bronte

Wuthering Heights is the name of Mr. Heathcliff's dwelling. 'Wuthering' being a significant provincial adjective, descriptive of the atmospheric tumult to which its station is exposed in stormy weather. Pure, bracing ventilation they must have up there at all times, indeed: one may guess the power of the north wind blowing over the edge, by the excessive slant of a few stunted firs at the end of the house; and by a range of gaunt thorns all stretching their limbs one way, as if craving alms of the sun. Happily, the architect had foresight to build it strong: the narrow windows are deeply set in the wall, and the corners defended with large jutting stones. Before passing the threshold, I paused to admire a quantity of grotesque carving lavished over the front, and especially about the principal door;

Pride and Prejudice by Jane Austen

An invitation to dinner was soon afterwards dispatched; and already had Mrs. Bennet planned the courses that were to do credit to her housekeeping, when an answer arrived which deferred it all. Mr. Bingley was obliged to be in town the following day, and, consequently, unable to accept the honour of their invitation, etc. Mrs. Bennet was quite disconcerted. She could not imagine what business he could have in town so soon after his arrival in Hertfordshire; and she began to fear that he might be always flying about from one place to another, and never settled at Netherfield as he ought to be. Lady Lucas quieted her fears a little by starting the idea of his being gone to London only to get a large party for the ball; and a report soon followed that Mr. Bingley was to bring twelve ladies and seven gentlemen

Alice's Adventures in Wonderland

by Lewis Carroll

There was nothing so VERY remarkable in that; nor did Alice think it so VERY much out of the way to hear the Rabbit say to itself, 'Oh dear! Oh dear! I shall be late!' (when she thought it over afterwards, it occurred to her that she ought to have wondered at this, but at the time it all seemed quite natural); but when the Rabbit actually TOOK A WATCH OUT OF ITS WAISTCOAT-POCKET, and looked at it, and then hurried on, Alice started to her feet, for it flashed across her mind that she had never before seen a rabbit with either a waistcoat pocket, or a watch to take out of it, and burning with curiosity, she ran across the field after it, and fortunately was just in time to see it pop down a large rabbit-hole under the hedge. In another moment down went Alice after it, never once considering how in the world she was to get out again. The

Moby Dick By Herman Melville

Call me Ishmael. Some years ago—never mind how long precisely—having little or no money in my purse, and nothing particular to interest me on shore, I thought I would sail about a little and see the watery part of the world. It is a way I have of driving off the spleen and regulating the circulation. Whenever I find myself growing grim about the mouth; whenever it is a damp, drizzly November in my soul; whenever I find myself involuntarily pausing before coffin warehouses, and bringing up the rear of every funeral I meet; and especially whenever my hypos get such an upper hand of me, that it requires a strong moral principle to prevent me from deliberately stepping into the street, and methodically knocking people's hats off—then, I account it high time to get to sea as soon as I can. This is my substitute for pistol

The Adventures of Sherlock Holmes

by Arthur Conan Doyle

To Sherlock Holmes she is always the woman. I have seldom heard him mention her under any other name. In his eyes she eclipses and predominates the whole of her sex. It was not that he felt any emotion akin to love for Irene Adler. All emotions, and that one particularly, were abhorrent to his cold, precise but admirably balanced mind. He was, I take it, the most perfect reasoning and observing machine that the world has seen, but as a lover he would have placed himself in a false position. He never spoke of the softer passions, save with a gibe and a sneer. They were admirable things for the observer—excellent for drawing the veil from men's motives and actions. But for the trained reasoner to admit such intrusions into his own delicate and finely adjusted temperament was to introduce a distracting factor which might throw a doubt upon all his

The Adventures of Tom Sawyer by Mark Twain

Aunt Polly was vexed to think she had overlooked that bit of circumstantial evidence, and missed a trick. Then she had a new inspiration: "Tom, you didn't have to undo your shirt collar where I sewed it, to pump on your head, did you? Unbutton your jacket!" The trouble vanished out of Tom's face. He opened his jacket. His shirt collar was securely sewed. "Bother! Well, go 'long with you. I'd made sure you'd played hookey and been a- swimming. But I forgive ye, Tom. I reckon you're a kind of a singed cat, as the saying is better'n you look. This time." She was half sorry her sagacity had miscarried, and half glad that Tom had stumbled into obedient conduct for once. But Sidney said: "Well, now, if I didn't think you sewed his collar with white thread, but it's black." "Why, I did sew it with white! Tom!" But Tom did not wait for

---

Redacted Poetry Journal

Dracula by Bram Stoker

All day long we seemed to dawdle through a country which was full of beauty of every kind. Sometimes we saw little towns or castles on the top of steep hills such as we see in old missals; sometimes we ran by rivers and streams which seemed from the wide stony margin on each side of them to be subject to great floods. It takes a lot of water, and running strong, to sweep the outside edge of a river clear. At every station there were groups of people, sometimes crowds, and in all sorts of attire. Some of them were just like the peasants at home or those I saw coming through France and Germany, with short jackets and round hats and home-made trousers; but others were very picturesque. The women looked pretty, except when you got near them, but they were very clumsy about the waist. They had all full white sleeves of some kind or other, and most

A Tale of Two Cities by Charles Dickens

In England, there was scarcely an amount of order and protection to justify much national boasting. Daring burglaries by armed men, and highway robberies, took place in the capital itself every night; families were publicly cautioned not to go out of town without removing their furniture to upholsterers' warehouses for security; the highwayman in the dark was a City tradesman in the light, and, being recognised and challenged by his fellow-tradesman whom he stopped in his character of "the Captain," gallantly shot him through the head and rode away; the mail was waylaid by seven robbers, and the guard shot three dead, and then got shot dead himself by the other four, "in consequence of the failure of his ammunition:" after which the mail was robbed in peace; that magnificent potentate, the

Heart of Darkness by Joseph Conrad

And at last, in its curved and imperceptible fall, the sun sank low, and from glowing white changed to a dull red without rays and without heat, as if about to go out suddenly, stricken to death by the touch of that gloom brooding over a crowd of men. Forthwith a change came over the waters, and the serenity became less brilliant but more profound. The old river in its broad reach rested unruffled at the decline of day, after ages of good service done to the race that peopled its banks, spread out in the tranquil dignity of a waterway leading to the uttermost ends of the earth. We looked at the venerable stream not in the vivid flush of a short day that comes and departs forever, but in the august light of abiding memories. And indeed nothing is easier for a man who has, as the phrase goes, followed the sea with reverence and affection

The Golden Bird, Grimm's Fairy Tales

by The Brothers Grimm

A certain king had a beautiful garden, and in the garden stood a tree which bore golden apples. These apples were always counted, and about the time when they began to grow ripe it was found that every night one of them was gone. The king became very angry at this, and ordered the gardener to keep watch all night under the tree. The gardener set his eldest son to watch; but about twelve o'clock he fell asleep, and in the morning another of the apples was missing. Then the second son was ordered to watch; and at midnight he too fell asleep, and in the morning another apple was gone. Then the third son offered to keep watch; but the gardener at first would not let him, for fear some harm should come to him: however, at last he consented, and the young man laid himself under the tree to watch. As the clock struck twelve he heard a rustling

The Iliad of Homer by Homer

Thus o'er the field the moving host appears, With nodding plumes and groves of waving spears. The gathering murmur spreads, their trampling feet Beat the loose sands, and thicken to the fleet; With long- resounding cries they urge the train To fit the ships, and launch into the main. They toil, they sweat, thick clouds of dust arise, The doubling clamours echo to the skies. E'en then the Greeks had left the hostile plain, And fate decreed the fall of Troy in vain; But Jove's imperial queen their flight survey'd, And sighing thus bespoke the blue-eyed maid: "Shall then the Grecians fly! O dire disgrace! And leave unpunish'd this perfidious race? Shall Troy, shall Priam, and the adulterous spouse, In peace enjoy the fruits of broken vows? And bravest chiefs, in Helen's quarrel slain, Lie unrevenged on yon detested plain? No:

War and Peace by Leo Tolstoy

Prince Vasíli always spoke languidly, like an actor repeating a stale part. Anna Pávlovna Schérer on the contrary, despite her forty years, overflowed with animation and impulsiveness. To be an enthusiast had become her social vocation and, sometimes even when she did not feel like it, she became enthusiastic in order not to disappoint the expectations of those who knew her. The subdued smile which, though it did not suit her faded features, always played round her lips expressed, as in a spoiled child, a continual consciousness of her charming defect, which she neither wished, nor could, nor considered it necessary, to correct. In the midst of a conversation on political matters Anna Pávlovna burst out: "Oh, don't speak to me of Austria. Perhaps I don't understand things, but Austria never has wished, and does not wish, for

Frankenstein by Mary Wollstonecraft Shelley

His daughter attended him with the greatest tenderness, but she saw with despair that their little fund was rapidly decreasing and that there was no other prospect of support. But Caroline Beaufort possessed a mind of an uncommon mould, and her courage rose to support her in her adversity. She procured plain work; she plaited straw and by various means contrived to earn a pittance scarcely sufficient to support life. Several months passed in this manner. Her father grew worse; her time was more entirely occupied in attending him; her means of subsistence decreased; and in the tenth month her father died in her arms, leaving her an orphan and a beggar. This last blow overcame her, and she knelt by Beaufort's coffin weeping bitterly, when my father entered the chamber. He came like a protecting spirit to the poor girl, who committed

The Count of Monte Cristo

by Alexandre Dumas, père

Beyond a bare, weather-worn wall, about a hundred paces from the spot where the two friends sat looking and listening as they drank their wine, was the village of the Catalans. Long ago this mysterious colony quitted Spain and settled on the tongue of land on which it is to this day. Whence it came no one knew, and it spoke an unknown tongue. One of its chiefs, who understood Provençal, begged the commune of Marseilles to give them this bare and barren promontory, where, like the sailors of old, they had run their boats ashore. The request was granted; and three months afterwards, around the twelve or fifteen small vessels which had brought these gypsies of the sea, a small village sprang up. This village, constructed in a singular and picturesque manner, half Moorish, half Spanish, still remains, and is inhabit-

The Importance of Being Earnest: A Trivial Comedy for Serious People by Oscar Wilde

Jack. I fear there can be no possible doubt about the matter. This afternoon during my temporary absence in London on an important question of romance, he obtained admission to my house by means of the false pretence of being my brother. Under an assumed name he drank, I've just been informed by my butler, an entire pint bottle of my Perrier-Jouet, Brut, '89; wine I was specially reserving for myself. Continuing his disgraceful deception, he succeeded in the course of the afternoon in alienating the affections of my only ward. He subsequently stayed to tea, and devoured every single muffin. And what makes his conduct all the more heartless is, that he was perfectly well aware from the first that I have no brother, that I never had a brother, and that I don't intend to have a brother, not even of any kind. I distinctly told him so

The Fall of the House of Usher

by Edgar Allan Poe

During the whole of a dull, dark, and soundless day in the autumn of the year, when the clouds hung oppressively low in the heavens, I had been passing alone, on horseback, through a singularly dreary tract of country, and at length found myself, as the shades of the evening drew on, within view of the melancholy House of Usher. I know not how it was—but, with the first glimpse of the building, a sense of insufferable gloom pervaded my spirit. I say insufferable; for the feeling was unrelieved by any of that half-pleasurable, because poetic, sentiment, with which the mind usually receives even the sternest natural images of the desolate or terrible. I looked upon the scene before me— upon the mere house, and the simple landscape features of the domain—upon the bleak walls—upon the vacant eye-like windows—upon a few rank

This Side of Paradise by F. Scott Fitzgerald

Before he was summoned back to Lake Geneva, he had appeared, shy but inwardly glowing, in his first long trousers, set off by a purple accordion tie and a "Belmont" collar with the edges unassailably meeting, purple socks, and handkerchief with a purple border peeping from his breast pocket. But more than that, he had formulated his first philosophy, a code to live by, which, as near as it can be named, was a sort of aristocratic egotism. He had realized that his best interests were bound up with those of a certain variant, changing person, whose label, in order that his past might always be identified with him, was Amory Blaine. Amory marked himself a fortunate youth, capable of infinite expansion for good or evil. He did not consider himself a "strong char'c'ter," but relied on his facility (learn things sorta quick) and

Les Misérables by Victor Hugo

Although this detail has no connection whatever with the real substance of what we are about to relate, it will not be superfluous, if merely for the sake of exactness in all points, to mention here the various rumors and remarks which had been in circulation about him from the very moment when he arrived in the diocese. True or false, that which is said of men often occupies as important a place in their lives, and above all in their destinies, as that which they do. M. Myriel was the son of a councillor of the Parliament of Aix; hence he belonged to the nobility of the bar. It was said that his father, destining him to be the heir of his own post, had married him at a very early age, eighteen or twenty, in accordance with a custom which is rather widely prevalent in parliamentary families. In spite of this marriage, however, it was said that Charles Myriel

Paradise Lost by John Milton

Fall'n Cherube, to be weak is miserable Doing or Suffering: but of this be sure, To do ought good never will be our task, But ever to do ill our sole delight, As being the contrary to his high will Whom we resist. If then his Providence Out of our evil seek to bring forth good, Our labour must be to pervert that end, And out of good still to find means of evil; Which oft times may succeed, so as perhaps Shall grieve him, if I fail not, and disturb His inmost counsels from their destind aim. But see the angry Victor hath recall'd His Ministers of vengeance and pursuit Back to the Gates of Heav'n: The Sulphurous Hail Shot after us in storm, oreblown hath laid The fiery Surge, that from the Precipice Of Heav'n receiv'd us falling, and the Thunder, Wing'd with red Lightning and impetuous rage, Perhaps hath spent his shafts, and ceases now To bellow through

Gulliver's Travels by Jonathan Swift

I hope you will be ready to own publicly, whenever you shall be called to it, that by your great and frequent urgency you prevailed on me to publish a very loose and uncorrect account of my travels, with directions to hire some young gentleman of either university to put them in order, and correct the style, as my cousin Dampier did, by my advice, in his book called "A Voyage round the world." But I do not remember I gave you power to consent that any thing should be omitted, and much less that any thing should be inserted; therefore, as to the latter, I do here renounce every thing of that kind; particularly a paragraph about her majesty Queen Anne, of most pious and glorious memory; although I did reverence and esteem her more than any of human species. But you, or your interpolator, ought to have considered, that it was not my inclin-

The Call of the Wild by Jack London

Buck did not read the newspapers, or he would have known that trouble was brewing, not alone for himself, but for every tide-water dog, strong of muscle and with warm, long hair, from Puget Sound to San Diego. Because men, groping in the Arctic darkness, had found a yellow metal, and because steamship and transportation companies were booming the find, thousands of men were rushing into the Northland. These men wanted dogs, and the dogs they wanted were heavy dogs, with strong muscles by which to toil, and furry coats to protect them from the frost. Buck lived at a big house in the sun-kissed Santa Clara Valley. Judge Miller's place, it was called. It stood back from the road, half hidden among the trees, through which glimpses could be caught of the wide cool veranda that ran around its four sides. The house was approached by gravelled drive-

Hamlet by William Shakespeare

Though yet of Hamlet our dear brother's death The memory be green, and that it us befitted To bear our hearts in grief, and our whole kingdom To be contracted in one brow of woe; Yet so far hath discretion fought with nature That we with wisest sorrow think on him, Together with remembrance of ourselves. Therefore our sometime sister, now our queen, Th'imperial jointress to this warlike state, Have we, as 'twere with a defeated joy, With one auspicious and one dropping eye, With mirth in funeral, and with dirge in marriage, In equal scale weighing delight and dole, Taken to wife; nor have we herein barr'd Your better wisdoms, which have freely gone With this affair along. For all, our thanks. Now follows, that you know young Fortinbras, Holding a weak supposal of our worth, Or thinking by our late dear brother's death Our state to be disjoint

***Anthem* by Ayn Rand**

It is a sin to write this. It is a sin to think words no others think and to put them down upon a paper no others are to see. It is base and evil. It is as if we were speaking alone to no ears but our own. And we know well that there is no transgression blacker than to do or think alone. We have broken the laws. The laws say that men may not write unless the Council of Vocations bid them so. May we be forgiven! But this is not the only sin upon us. We have committed a greater crime, and for this crime there is no name. What punishment awaits us if it be discovered we know not, for no such crime has come in the memory of men and there are no laws to provide for it. It is dark here. The flame of the candle stands still in the air. Nothing moves in this tunnel save our hand on the paper. We are alone here under the earth. It is a fearful word, alone. The

The Tale of Peter Rabbit by Beatrix Potter

Mr. McGregor was on his hands and knees planting out young cabbages, but he jumped up and ran after Peter, waving a rake and calling out, 'Stop thief!' Peter was most dreadfully frightened; he rushed all over the garden, for he had forgotten the way back to the gate. He lost one of his shoes among the cabbages, and the other shoe amongst the potatoes. After losing them, he ran on four legs and went faster, so that I think he might have got away altogether if he had not unfortunately run into a gooseberry net, and got caught by the large buttons on his jacket. It was a blue jacket with brass buttons, quite new. Peter gave himself up for lost, and shed big tears; but his sobs were overheard by some friendly sparrows, who flew to him in great excitement, and implored him to exert himself. Mr. McGregor came up with a sieve, which he

Around the World in 80 Days by Jules Verne

He suddenly observed, hung over the clock, a card which, upon inspection, proved to be a programme of the daily routine of the house. It comprised all that was required of the servant, from eight in the morning, exactly at which hour Phileas Fogg rose, till half-past eleven, when he left the house for the Reform Club—all the details of service, the tea and toast at twenty-three minutes past eight, the shaving-water at thirty-seven minutes past nine, and the toilet at twenty minutes before ten. Everything was regulated and foreseen that was to be done from half-past eleven a.m. till midnight, the hour at which the methodical gentleman retired. Mr. Fogg's wardrobe was amply supplied and in the best taste. Each pair of trousers, coat, and vest bore a number, indicating the time of year and season at which they were in turn to be laid

Utopia by Thomas More

If any man has a mind to visit his friends that live in some other town, or desires to travel and see the rest of the country, he obtains leave very easily from the Syphogrant and Tranibors, when there is no particular occasion for him at home. Such as travel carry with them a passport from the Prince, which both certifies the licence that is granted for travelling, and limits the time of their return. They are furnished with a waggon and a slave, who drives the oxen and looks after them; but, unless there are women in the company, the waggon is sent back at the end of the journey as a needless encumbrance. While they are on the road they carry no provisions with them, yet they want for nothing, but are everywhere treated as if they were at home. If they stay in any place longer than a night, every one follows

Twelve Years a Slave by Solomon Northup

Though born a slave, and laboring under the disadvantages to which my unfortunate race is subjected, my father was a man respected for his industry and integrity, as many now living, who well remember him, are ready to testify. His whole life was passed in the peaceful pursuits of agriculture, never seeking employment in those more menial positions, which seem to be especially allotted to the children of Africa. Besides giving us an education surpassing that ordinarily bestowed upon children in our condition, he acquired, by his diligence and economy, a sufficient property qualification to entitle him to the right of suffrage. He was accustomed to speak to us of his early life; and although at all times cherishing the warmest emotions of kindness, and even of affection towards the family, in whose house he had been

The Almost-Men by Irving E. Cox

Pendillo's sons were naked, then, except for their short, crudely cut breeches and their leather weapon belts. And only the belts, which held their stone knives and their clubs, would either of them have considered essential. The rest was superficial, a mark of status. In a general way Lanny and Gill were physically alike—sturdy, bronzed giants, like all the children who had survived in the treaty areas. They were both nineteen, or perhaps a little older. Dr. Pendillo had found them abandoned as he fled the final enemy attack. Gill's hair was yellow and a pale beard was beginning to grow on his chin. Lanny's black hair curled in a tight, matted mane; his beard was heavy, already covering much of his face and giving him a sinister, derelict appearance. Since metal was forbidden in the prison compounds, no man was clean-

The Waste Land by T. S. Eliot

Under the brown fog of a winter noon Mr. Eugenides, the Smyrna merchant Unshaven, with a pocket full of currants C.i.f. London: documents at sight, Asked me in demotic French To luncheon at the Cannon Street Hotel Followed by a weekend at the Metropole. At the violet hour, when the eyes and back Turn upward from the desk, when the human engine waits Like a taxi throbbing waiting, I Tiresias, though blind, throbbing between two lives, Old man with wrinkled female breasts, can see At the violet hour, the evening hour that strives Homeward, and brings the sailor home from sea, The typist home at teatime, clears her breakfast, lights Her stove, and lays out food in tins. Out of the window perilously spread Her drying combinations touched by the sun's last rays, On the divan are piled (at night her bed) Stockings, slippers, camisoles,

The Secret Garden

by Frances Hodgson Burnett

When he shut the door, mounted the box with the coachman, and they drove off, the little girl found herself seated in a comfortably cushioned corner, but she was not inclined to go to sleep again. She sat and looked out of the window, curious to see something of the road over which she was being driven to the queer place Mrs. Medlock had spoken of. She was not at all a timid child and she was not exactly frightened, but she felt that there was no knowing what might happen in a house with a hundred rooms nearly all shut up—a house standing on the edge of a moor. What is a moor?" she said suddenly to Mrs. Medlock. Look out of the window in about ten minutes and you'll see," the woman answered. "We've got to drive five miles across Missel Moor before we get to the Manor. You won't see much because it's a dark night, but you can see something." Mary

Resources & Info

VISIT: Stop by **www.offbeatpoet.com** for writing resources, tools, and tips.

SHARE: Post your redacted works on social to connect with other creators. Don't forget to tag me!

CONNECT:

www.offbeatpoet.com

| offbeatpoet | offbeatpoet1 | offbeatpoet | obeatpoet |

#offbeatpoetry
#redactedpoetry

Redacted Poetry Journal: *Create Blackout Poetry by Destroying the Classics* is available in both digital and print editions. Try redacting both versions to stretch your creativity! www.RedactedPoetry.com

Redacted Poetry Journal

Made in the USA
Middletown, DE
31 July 2019